# every day
## MATTERS
### 2016 DIARY

*Lala Li Donni*

A YEAR OF INSPIRATION
FOR THE MIND, BODY & SPIRIT

in association with KINDRED

Every Day Matters 2016 Diary

First published in UK and USA in 2015 by
Watkins, an imprint of Watkins Media Limited
19 Cecil Court, London WC2N 4EZ
enquiries@watkinspublishing.co.uk

Designed by Watkins Media Limited

Author/Illustrator: Dani DiPirro
Art Direction: Georgina Hewitt
Designer: Sophie Yamamoto
Commissioning Editor: Kelly Thompson
Managing Editor: Deborah Hercun
Editor: Judy Barratt

Desk Diary ISBN: 978-1-78028-834-5
Pocket Diary ISBN: 978-1-78028-835-2

Colour reproduction by XY Digital, UK
Printed in China

Phases of the Moon:
- ● New moon
- ☽ First quarter
- ○ Full moon
- ☾ Last quarter

Signs of the Zodiac:

| ♈ | Aries | March 21–April 20 |
|---|---|---|
| ♉ | Taurus | April 21–May 20 |
| ♊ | Gemini | May 21–June 21 |
| ♋ | Cancer | June 22–July 22 |
| ♌ | Leo | July 23–August 23 |
| ♍ | Virgo | August 24–September 23 |
| ♎ | Libra | September 24–October 23 |
| ♏ | Scorpio | October 24–November 22 |
| ♐ | Sagittarius | November 23–December 21 |
| ♑ | Capricorn | December 22–January 20 |
| ♒ | Aquarius | January 21–February 19 |
| ♓ | Pisces | February 20–March 20 |

Abbreviations:
BCE: Before Common Era (equivalent of BC)
CE: Common Era (equivalent of AD)

UK: United Kingdom
SCO: Scotland
NIR: Northern Ireland
ROI: Republic of Ireland
CAN: Canada
USA: United States of America
NZ: New Zealand
AUS: Australia
ACT: Australian Capital Territory
NSW: New South Wales
NT: Northern Territory
QLD: Queensland
SA: South Australia
TAS: Tasmania
VIC: Victoria
WA: Western Australia

Publisher's Notes:
All dates relating to the zodiac signs and the phases of the moon
are based on Greenwich Mean Time (GMT).

All North American holiday dates are based on Eastern Standard
Time (EST).

Jewish and Islamic holidays begin at sundown on the date
given. Islamic holidays may vary by a day or two, as the Islamic
calendar is based on a combination of actual sightings of the
moon and astronomical calculations.

Note on Public Holidays:
Holiday dates were correct at the time of going to press.

# 2015

| JANUARY | FEBRUARY | MARCH | APRIL | MAY | JUNE |
|---|---|---|---|---|---|
| M TU W TH F SA SU | M TU W TH F SA SU | M TU W TH F SA SU | M TU W TH F SA SU | M TU W TH F SA SU | M TU W TH F SA SU |
| 1 2 3 4 | 1 | 1 | 1 2 3 4 5 | 1 2 3 | 1 2 3 4 5 6 7 |
| 5 6 7 8 9 10 11 | 2 3 4 5 6 7 8 | 2 3 4 5 6 7 8 | 6 7 8 9 10 11 12 | 4 5 6 7 8 9 10 | 8 9 10 11 12 13 14 |
| 12 13 14 15 16 17 18 | 9 10 11 12 13 14 15 | 9 10 11 12 13 14 15 | 13 14 15 16 17 18 19 | 11 12 13 14 15 16 17 | 15 16 17 18 19 20 21 |
| 19 20 21 22 23 24 25 | 16 17 18 19 20 21 22 | 16 17 18 19 20 21 22 | 20 21 22 23 24 25 26 | 18 19 20 21 22 23 24 | 22 23 24 25 26 27 28 |
| 26 27 28 29 30 31 | 23 24 25 26 27 28 | 23 24 25 26 27 28 29 | 27 28 29 30 | 25 26 27 28 (29) 30 31 | 29 30 |
| | | 30 31 | | | |

| JULY | AUGUST | SEPTEMBER | OCTOBER | NOVEMBER | DECEMBER |
|---|---|---|---|---|---|
| M TU W TH F SA SU | M TU W TH F SA SU | M TU W TH F SA SU | M TU W TH F SA SU | M TU W TH F SA SU | M TU W TH F SA SU |
| 1 2 3 4 5 | 1 2 | 1 2 3 4 5 6 | 1 2 3 4 | 1 | 1 2 3 4 5 6 |
| 6 7 8 9 10 11 12 | 3 4 5 6 7 8 9 | 7 8 9 10 11 12 13 | 5 6 7 8 9 10 11 | 2 3 4 5 6 7 8 | 7 8 9 10 11 12 13 |
| 13 14 15 16 17 18 19 | 10 11 12 13 14 15 16 | 14 15 16 17 18 19 20 | 12 13 14 15 16 17 18 | 9 10 11 12 13 14 15 | 14 15 16 17 18 19 20 |
| 20 21 22 23 24 25 26 | 17 18 19 20 21 22 23 | 21 22 23 24 25 26 27 | 19 20 21 22 23 24 25 | 16 17 18 19 20 21 22 | 21 22 23 24 25 26 27 |
| 27 28 29 30 31 | 24 25 26 27 28 29 30 | 28 29 30 | 26 27 28 29 30 31 | 23 24 25 26 27 28 29 | 28 29 30 31 |
| | 31 | | | 30 | |

# 2016

| JANUARY | FEBRUARY | MARCH | APRIL |
|---|---|---|---|
| M TU W TH F SA SU | M TU W TH F SA SU | M TU W TH F SA SU | M TU W TH F SA SU |
| 1 2 3 | 1 2 3 4 5 6 7 | 1 2 3 4 5 6 | 1 2 3 |
| 4 5 6 7 8 9 10 | 8 9 10 11 12 13 14 | 7 8 9 10 11 12 13 | 4 5 6 7 8 9 10 |
| 11 12 13 14 15 16 17 | 15 16 17 18 19 20 21 | 14 15 16 17 18 19 20 | 11 12 13 14 15 16 17 |
| 18 19 20 21 22 23 24 | 22 23 24 25 26 27 28 | 21 22 23 24 25 26 27 | 18 19 20 21 22 23 24 |
| 25 26 27 28 29 30 31 | 29 | 28 29 30 31 | 25 26 27 28 29 30 |

| MAY | JUNE | JULY | AUGUST |
|---|---|---|---|
| M TU W TH F SA SU | M TU W TH F SA SU | M TU W TH F SA SU | M TU W TH F SA SU |
| 1 | 1 2 3 4 5 | 1 2 3 | 1 2 3 4 5 6 7 |
| 2 3 4 5 6 7 8 | 6 7 8 9 10 11 12 | 4 5 6 7 8 9 10 | 8 9 10 11 12 13 14 |
| 9 10 11 12 13 14 15 | 13 14 15 16 17 18 19 | 11 12 13 14 15 16 17 | 15 16 17 18 19 20 21 |
| 16 17 18 19 20 21 22 | 20 21 22 23 24 25 26 | 18 19 20 21 22 23 24 | 22 23 24 25 26 27 28 |
| 23 24 25 26 27 28 (29) | 27 28 29 30 | 25 26 27 28 29 30 31 | 29 30 31 |
| 30 31 | | | |

| SEPTEMBER | OCTOBER | NOVEMBER | DECEMBER |
|---|---|---|---|
| M TU W TH F SA SU | M TU W TH F SA SU | M TU W TH F SA SU | M TU W TH F SA SU |
| 1 2 3 4 | 1 2 | 1 2 3 4 5 6 | 1 2 3 4 |
| 5 6 7 8 9 10 11 | 3 4 5 6 7 8 9 | 7 8 9 10 11 12 13 | 5 6 7 8 9 10 11 |
| 12 13 14 15 16 17 18 | 10 11 12 13 14 15 16 | 14 15 16 17 18 19 20 | 12 13 14 15 16 17 18 |
| 19 20 21 22 23 24 25 | 17 18 19 20 21 22 23 | 21 22 23 24 25 26 27 | 19 20 21 22 23 24 25 |
| 26 27 28 29 30 | 24 25 26 27 28 29 30 | 28 29 30 | 26 27 28 29 30 31 |
| | 31 | | |

# 2017

| JANUARY | FEBRUARY | MARCH | APRIL | MAY | JUNE |
|---|---|---|---|---|---|
| M TU W TH F SA SU | M TU W TH F SA SU | M TU W TH F SA SU | M TU W TH F SA SU | M TU W TH F SA SU | M TU W TH F SA SU |
| 1 | 1 2 3 4 5 | 1 2 3 4 5 | 1 2 | 1 2 3 4 5 6 7 | 1 2 3 4 |
| 2 3 4 5 6 7 8 | 6 7 8 9 10 11 12 | 6 7 8 9 10 11 12 | 3 4 5 6 7 8 9 | 8 9 10 11 12 13 14 | 5 6 7 8 9 10 11 |
| 9 10 11 12 13 14 15 | 13 14 15 16 17 18 19 | 13 14 15 16 17 18 19 | 10 11 12 13 14 15 16 | 15 16 17 18 19 20 21 | 12 13 14 15 16 17 18 |
| 16 17 18 19 20 21 22 | 20 21 22 23 24 25 26 | 20 21 22 23 24 25 26 | 17 18 19 20 21 22 23 | 22 23 24 25 26 27 28 | 19 20 21 22 23 24 25 |
| 23 24 25 26 27 28 29 | 27 28 | 27 28 29 30 31 | 24 25 26 27 28 (29) 30 31 | 29 30 31 | 26 27 28 29 30 |
| 30 31 | | | | | |

| JULY | AUGUST | SEPTEMBER | OCTOBER | NOVEMBER | DECEMBER |
|---|---|---|---|---|---|
| M TU W TH F SA SU | M TU W TH F SA SU | M TU W TH F SA SU | M TU W TH F SA SU | M TU W TH F SA SU | M TU W TH F SA SU |
| 1 2 | 1 2 3 4 5 6 | 1 2 3 | 1 | 1 2 3 4 5 | 1 2 3 |
| 3 4 5 6 7 8 9 | 7 8 9 10 11 12 13 | 4 5 6 7 8 9 10 | 2 3 4 5 6 7 8 | 6 7 8 9 10 11 12 | 4 5 6 7 8 9 10 |
| 10 11 12 13 14 15 16 | 14 15 16 17 18 19 20 | 11 12 13 14 15 16 17 | 9 10 11 12 13 14 15 | 13 14 15 16 17 18 19 | 11 12 13 14 15 16 17 |
| 17 18 19 20 21 22 23 | 21 22 23 24 25 26 27 | 18 19 20 21 22 23 24 | 16 17 18 19 20 21 22 | 20 21 22 23 24 25 26 | 18 19 20 21 22 23 24 |
| 24 25 26 27 28 29 30 | 28 29 30 31 | 25 26 27 28 29 30 | 23 24 25 26 27 28 29 | 27 28 29 30 | 25 26 27 28 29 30 31 |
| 31 | | | 30 31 | | |

| | |
|---|---|
| Argentina | Jan. 1, Feb. 8-9, Mar. 25, Apr. 2, May 1, May 25, June 20, July 9, Aug. 15, Oct. 10, Nov. 28, Dec. 8, Dec. 25 |
| Australia | Jan. 1, Jan. 26, Mar. 14 (ACT, SA, TAS, VIC), Mar. 25, Mar. 28, Apr. 25, June 13 (ACT, NSW, NT, QLD, SA, TAS, VIC), Oct. 3 (ACT, NSW, QLD, SA), Dec. 25-27 |
| Austria | Jan. 1, Jan. 6, Mar.28, May 5, May 16, May 26, Aug. 15, Oct. 26, Nov. 1, Dec. 8, Dec. 25-26 |
| Belgium | Jan. 1, Mar.28, May 5, May 16, July 21, Aug. 15, Nov. 1, Nov. 11, Dec. 25 |
| Brazil | Jan. 1, Feb. 8-10, Mar.25, Apr.21, May 1, May 26, May 1, Sep. 7, Oct. 12, Nov. 2, Nov. 15, Nov. 20, Dec. 25 |
| Canada | Jan. 1, Mar. 25, Mar. 28 (AB, BC, NB, PE, QC, YT), May 23, July 1, Sep. 5, Oct. 10, Nov. 11, Dec. 25 |
| China | Jan. 1, Feb. 7-13, Apr. 4, May 1, June 9, Sep. 15, Oct. 1-7, Oct. 9 |
| Denmark | Jan. 1, Mar. 24-25, Mar. 28, Apr. 22, May 5, May 16, June 5, Dec. 24, Dec. 25-26, Dec. 31 |
| Finland | Jan. 1, Jan. 6, Mar. 25, Mar. 28, May 1, May 5, June 24, June 25, Nov. 5, Dec. 6, Dec. 24-26 |
| France | Jan. 1, Mar. 28, May 1, May 5, May 8, May 16, July 14, Aug. 15, Nov. 1, Nov. 11, Dec. 25 |
| Germany | Jan. 1, Mar. 25, Mar. 28, May 1, May 5, May 16, Oct. 3, Nov. 1, Dec. 25-26 |
| Greece | Jan. 1, Jan. 6, Mar. 14, Mar. 25, Apr. 29, May 1-2, June 20, Aug. 15, Oct. 28, Dec. 25-26 |
| India | Jan. 26, Apr. 19, Aug. 15, Oct. 2, Oct. 11, Dec. 25 |
| Indonesia | Jan. 1, Feb. 7, Mar. 9, Mar. 25, May 1, May 5, May 21, July 7-8, Aug. 18, Sept. 11, Oct. 2, Dec. 25 |
| Israel | Mar. 24, Apr. 23, Apr. 29, May 12, June 12, Oct. 3-4, Oct. 12, Oct.17, Oct. 24 |
| Italy | Jan. 1, Jan. 6, Mar. 28, Apr. 25, May 1, June 2, Aug. 15, Nov. 1, Dec. 8, Dec. 25-26 |
| Japan | Jan. 1, Jan. 11, Feb. 11, Mar. 20, Apr. 29, May 3-5, July 18, Sep. 19, Sep. 22, Oct. 10, Nov. 3, Nov. 23, Dec. 23 |

| | |
|---|---|
| Luxembourg | Jan. 1, Mar. 25, Mar. 28, May 1, May 5, May 16, June 23, Aug. 15, Nov. 1, Dec. 25-26 |
| Mexico | Jan. 1, Feb. 1, Mar. 14, Mar. 21, Mar. 24, Mar. 25, May 1, Sep. 16, Nov. 2, Nov. 21, Dec. 12, Dec. 25-26 |
| Netherlands | Jan. 1, Mar. 25, Mar. 28, May 5, May 16, Dec. 25-26 |
| New Zealand | Jan. 1, Jan. 4, Feb. 8, Mar. 25, Mar. 28, Apr. 25, June 6, Oct. 24, Dec. 25-26, Dec. 27 |
| Nigeria | Jan. 1, Mar. 8, Mar. 25, Mar. 28, May 1, May 29, July 7, Sep. 11, Oct. 1, Dec. 24-27, Dec. 31 |
| Pakistan | Feb. 5, Mar. 23, May 1, July 7-9, Aug. 14, Sep. 11-12, Oct. 11, Nov. 9, Dec. 25 |
| Poland | Jan. 1, Jan. 6, Mar. 25, Mar. 27-28, May 1, May 3, May 15, May 26, Aug. 15, Nov. 1, Nov. 11, Dec. 25-26 |
| Portugal | Jan. 1, Mar. 25, Apr. 25, May 1, June 10, Aug. 15, Dec. 8, Dec. 24-25 |
| Republic of Ireland | Jan. 1, Mar. 17, Mar. 28, May 2, June 6, Aug. 1, Oct. 31, Dec. 25-27 |
| Russia | Jan. 1, Jan. 4-7, Feb. 23, Mar. 8, May 1, May 9, June 12, Nov. 4 |
| South Africa | Jan. 1, Jan. 6, Mar. 25, Mar. 28, Apr. 27, May 1, June 16, Aug. 9, Sep. 24, Dec. 16, Dec. 25-26 |
| Spain | Jan. 1, Jan. 6, Mar. 25, Mar. 28, May 1, Aug. 15, Oct. 12, Nov. 1, Dec. 6, Dec. 8, Dec. 25-26 |
| Sweden | Jan. 1, Jan. 6, Mar. 25, Mar. 28, May 1, May 5, June 6, June 24, Nov. 5, Dec. 24-26, Dec. 31 |
| Turkey | Jan. 1, Apr. 23, May 1, May 19, July 8-9, Aug. 30, Sep. 12-15, Oct. 29 |
| United Kingdom | Jan. 1, Mar. 25, Mar. 28, May 2, May 30, Aug. 29, Dec. 25-27 |
| United States | Jan. 1, Jan. 18, Feb. 15, May 30, July 4, Sep. 5, Oct. 10, Nov. 11, Nov. 24, Dec. 25-26 |

# HAPPY 2016!

Are you ready to start off the year with a positive vibe? Are you hoping to make the most of every single day? If so, you've picked up the right diary!

Every new year brings 365 days filled with opportunities for change, joy, love and happiness. Every month, week and day in this diary provides encouraging words from positivity writer Dani DiPirro, aimed at inspiring you to make the most of those opportunities. This is your year to seize every chance you have to focus on the most inspirational and joyful aspects of your life.

Dani has hand-picked this year's monthly themes – Happiness, Creativity, Truth, Beauty, Simplicity, Kindness, Mindfulness, Gratitude, Wisdom, Courage, Curiosity and Growth – and has captured the essence of each in inspirational quotations, empowering activities and thought-provoking reflections. At the start of every month, you'll also find a theme-related affirmation to keep in mind as you go about your daily life. And, of course, there's plenty of space to jot down your appointments and to-do lists, too.

May your 2016 be filled with 365 days that really matter!

# HAPPINESS

Welcome to 2016! The start of a new year is the perfect time to think about the one quality we all want more of in our lives: happiness. Ask yourself what makes you happy every day. What sensory experiences fill your world with light? Who brightens your face with a smile? What activities or pastimes make you feel the warmth of happiness soaking through you? Although you may not feel happy every moment of the year, it is possible to seek out the experiences and people that bring you closer to happiness every day. Just as a flower tilts its petals towards the sun, spend every day directing your actions towards moments that will make you happy.

## AFFIRMATION OF THE MONTH
*I choose happiness every day*

# DECEMBER 28 – JANUARY 3

*happiness*

28 / MONDAY

29 / TUESDAY

30 / WEDNESDAY

NOTES

*"Happiness is when what you think, what you say and what you do are in harmony."*

MAHATMA GANDHI, INDIAN LEADER (1869-1948)

## 31 / THURSDAY

New Year's Eve

## 1 / FRIDAY

New Year's Day
Kwanzaa ends

## 2 / SATURDAY ☾

## 3 / SUNDAY

### ACT ON POSITIVE THOUGHT

This week align your actions with positive thoughts.
Choose one task you don't love doing – such as the
laundry – and think of something positive about
it (maybe, "I love the way clean laundry smells").
Channel your positive thought into positive action,
to make a potentially onerous task a happier one.

# JANUARY 4 – JANUARY 10

*happiness*

## 4 / MONDAY

Public holiday (SCO, NZ)

## 5 / TUESDAY

## 6 / WEDNESDAY

Epiphany

## NOTES

*"Remember that very little is needed to make a happy life."*

MARCUS AURELIUS, ROMAN EMPEROR (121–180ce)

## 7 / THURSDAY

Christmas Day (Orthodox)

_____

_____

_____

_____

_____

_____

_____

_____

_____

## 8 / FRIDAY

_____

_____

_____

_____

_____

_____

_____

_____

_____

## 9 / SATURDAY

_____

_____

_____

_____

## 10 / SUNDAY ●

_____

_____

_____

_____

_____

### SIMPLIFY YOUR NEEDS

At the end of every day this week, write down three simple 'needs' for tomorrow that will bring you happiness. Make your ideas specific and achievable – a poached egg for breakfast, a call to your best friend, a hot bath before bedtime, and so on. Every new day make your three needs come true.

# JANUARY 11 - JANUARY 17

*happiness*

11 / MONDAY

12 / TUESDAY

13 / WEDNESDAY

NOTES

*"Happiness depends upon ourselves."*

ARISTOTLE, GREEK PHILOSOPHER (384–322BCE)

## 14 / THURSDAY

New Year's Day (Orthodox)

_____
_____
_____
_____
_____
_____
_____
_____
_____
_____
_____

## 15 / FRIDAY

_____
_____
_____
_____
_____
_____
_____
_____
_____
_____
_____

## 16 / SATURDAY ☽

_____
_____
_____
_____

## 17 / SUNDAY

_____
_____
_____
_____
_____
_____

## MAKE YOUR OWN BLISS

One lunchtime this week create your own moment of happiness by indulging in something you don't normally do - go to your favourite restaurant and order a coffee and a cake, buy yourself a flower (or a bunch of flowers), lie in the park and watch the clouds cross the sky.

# JANUARY 18 – JANUARY 24

*happiness*

### 18 / MONDAY

Martin Luther King, Jr. Day

### 19 / TUESDAY

### 20 / WEDNESDAY

NOTES

> *"A great obstacle to happiness is to expect too much happiness."*
>
> BERNARD LE BOVIER DE FONTENELLE, FRENCH AUTHOR (1657-1757)

## 21 / THURSDAY ≈

_____
_____
_____
_____
_____
_____
_____
_____
_____
_____

## 22 / FRIDAY

_____
_____
_____
_____
_____
_____
_____
_____
_____
_____

## 23 / SATURDAY

_____
_____
_____
_____

## 24 / SUNDAY ○

_____
_____
_____
_____
_____
_____

### SET FREE YOUR EXPECTATIONS

Expecting a certain outcome carries with it the potential for deep frustration. On your commute to work, consider your expectations for the day. Pick one and challenge it with this mantra: *Whatever the result, I will be happy.* When you feel the desire for an expected outcome creeping back in, repeat the mantra and let the expectation go.

# JANUARY 25 - JANUARY 31

*happiness*

### 25 / MONDAY

Burns' Night

### 26 / TUESDAY

Australia Day

### 27 / WEDNESDAY

Holocaust Memorial Day

## NOTES

*"I would always rather be happy than dignified."*
CHARLOTTE BRONTË, ENGLISH NOVELIST (1816–1855)

## 28 / THURSDAY

_____
_____
_____
_____
_____
_____
_____
_____
_____
_____

## 29 / FRIDAY

_____
_____
_____
_____
_____
_____
_____
_____
_____
_____

## 30 / SATURDAY

_____
_____
_____
_____

## 31 / SUNDAY

_____
_____
_____
_____
_____

### EMBRACE YOUR SILLY SIDE

Some of the happiest times are those in which we let go completely, embracing the freedom of not caring what others think. This week, choose to embrace happiness by doing one silly thing - skip along the pavement, sing as you walk or make funny faces at yourself in the mirror.

# JANUARY OVERVIEW

| M | TU | W | TH | F | SA | SU |
|---|----|----|----|----|----|----|
| 28 | 29 | 30 | 31 | 1 | 2 | 3 |
| 4 | 5 | 6 | 7 | 8 | 9 | 10 |
| 11 | 12 | 13 | 14 | 15 | 16 | 17 |
| 18 | 19 | 20 | 21 | 22 | 23 | 24 |
| 25 | 26 | 27 | 28 | 29 | 30 | 31 |

This month I am grateful for ...

_____

_____

_____

_____

_____

_____

_____

_____

# Reflections on HAPPINESS

In what ways did you focus on creating happiness in your life this month?

_____

_____

_____

_____

_____

_____

What aspects of your life bring you the most happiness?

_____

_____

_____

_____

_____

_____

What can you do throughout 2016 to continue to bring increased happiness into your life?

_____

_____

_____

_____

_____

_____

# FEBRUARY

# CREATIVITY

Creativity is abuzz in each one of us. Even if you don't consider yourself to be a creative person, you are. You have the power within you to breathe life into so many things - art, food, conversation, connections, relationships and more. You also have the power to create (or keep creating) the life you want to be living. Just as the bee floats from one flower to another, gathering pollen to make honey, you can find people, places and experiences that help you create a life that empowers and enriches who you are. This month, it's time to stop waiting for the "right moment" to begin and instead just get started. It's time to tap into the creativity within you and use your resourcefulness and imagination to create a month filled with joy, fulfilment and inspiration.

## AFFIRMATION OF THE MONTH
I create the life I want to live

# FEBRUARY 1 - FEBRUARY 7

*creativity*

### 1 / MONDAY ☾

St Brigid's Day (Imbolc)
Black History Month begins
(CAN/USA)

### 2 / TUESDAY

Groundhog Day
Candlemas

### 3 / WEDNESDAY

## NOTES

> "Every child is an artist. The problem is how to remain an artist once we grow up."
>
> PABLO PICASSO, SPANISH ARTIST (1881-1973)

## 4 / THURSDAY

## 5 / FRIDAY

## 6 / SATURDAY

Waitangi Day (NZ)

## 7 / SUNDAY

## WELCOME YOUR INNER CHILD

Children create in so many ways, from dressing up to scribbling pictures. One evening this week, turn off the TV and tap into your creative inner child - doodle with coloured pencils, paint a picture, sketch from a photograph. Don't judge the results - it's the act of creating that matters.

# FEBRUARY 8 – FEBRUARY 14

*creativity*

### 8 / MONDAY ●

Chinese New Year
(Year of the Monkey)
Losar (Tibetan New Year)
Waitangi Day (NZ)

### 9 / TUESDAY

Shrove Tuesday

### 10 / WEDNESDAY

Ash Wednesday

## NOTES

*"Creativity takes courage."*
HENRI MATISSE, FRENCH ARTIST (1869-1954)

## 11 / THURSDAY

_____
_____
_____
_____
_____
_____
_____
_____
_____
_____

## 12 / FRIDAY

Abraham Lincoln's birthday

_____
_____
_____
_____
_____
_____
_____
_____
_____
_____

## 13 / SATURDAY

_____
_____
_____
_____

## 14 / SUNDAY

St Valentine's Day

_____
_____
_____
_____
_____

### CREATE NEW EXPERIENCES

Many of us avoid new experiences because we're afraid to step beyond our comfort zones. Every day this week do something that takes a tiny bit of courage. On Monday invite someone you'd like to know better for coffee; on Tuesday try a new cuisine; on Wednesday walk down a street you've never visited before …

# FEBRUARY 15 – FEBRUARY 21

*creativity*

**15 / MONDAY** ☽

Presidents' Day / George
Washington's birthday (USA)

**16 / TUESDAY**

**17 / WEDNESDAY**

## NOTES

"Creating is the true essence of life."
BARTHOLD GEORG NIEBUHR, DANISH-GERMAN STATESMAN (1776-1831)

18 / THURSDAY

19 / FRIDAY

20 / SATURDAY ♓

21 / SUNDAY

### MAKE SOMETHING NEW

Upcycle something you own or create something from scratch - put up a shelf, sew a tote bag, paint a window frame. The project doesn't need to be complex, but as you do it revel in how enlivening it feels to create something new or to breathe new life into something old or worn.

# FEBRUARY 22 - FEBRUARY 28

*creativity*

**22 / MONDAY** ○

**23 / TUESDAY**

**24 / WEDNESDAY**

NOTES

*"But, if you have nothing at all to create, then perhaps you create yourself."*

CARL GUSTAV JUNG, SWISS PSYCHIATRIST (1875-1961)

## 25 / THURSDAY

## 26 / FRIDAY

## 27 / SATURDAY

## 28 / SUNDAY

### FIND YOUR BEST SELF

You are the hero of your own life story. This week make a list, with examples, of how you manifest your heroic qualities. Perhaps you are the organizer at home, the innovator at work and the good listener among your friends. In what practical ways can you cross-pollinate those qualities in every area of your life to create an even better version of yourself?

# FEBRUARY OVERVIEW

| M | TU | W | TH | F | SA | SU |
|---|----|----|----|----|----|----|
| 1 | 2 | 3 | 4 | 5 | 6 | 7 |
| 8 | 9 | 10 | 11 | 12 | 13 | 14 |
| 15 | 16 | 17 | 18 | 19 | 20 | 21 |
| 22 | 23 | 24 | 25 | 26 | 27 | 28 |
| 29 | 1 | 2 | 3 | 4 | 5 | 6 |

This month I am grateful for ...

_____

_____

_____

_____

_____

_____

_____

_____

# Reflections on CREATIVITY

What creative choices did you make in your life this month?

_____

_____

_____

_____

_____

_____

How did it feel to think and act more creatively over the past few weeks?

_____

_____

_____

_____

_____

_____

How can you cultivate more creativity in your life in the future?

_____

_____

_____

_____

_____

_____

MARCH

# TRUTH

Truth is a powerful tool - and staying true to yourself is one of the best ways to make the most of every moment, to feel you are living a fulfilled and honest life that you can be proud of. Your personal truth presents itself in little ways every day, with every action you take and even every word you speak - just as the little fronds of a fern unfurl little by little in the sunlight. This month is all about discovering the truth that lies within you. Every week offers a new way to reconnect with what matters most to you and encourages you to manifest your truth in your daily life.

## AFFIRMATION OF THE MONTH

*I choose to stay close to my truth*

# FEBRUARY 29 – MARCH 6

*truth*

**29 / MONDAY**

**1 / TUESDAY** ☽

St David's Day

**2 / WEDNESDAY**

NOTES

> *"All truths are easy to understand once they are discovered; the point is to discover them."*
>
> GALILEO GALILEI, ITALIAN PHYSICIST (1564-1642)

## 3 / THURSDAY

_____
_____
_____
_____
_____
_____
_____
_____
_____
_____
_____

## 4 / FRIDAY

_____
_____
_____
_____
_____
_____
_____
_____
_____
_____
_____

## 5 / SATURDAY

_____
_____
_____
_____

## 6 / SUNDAY

Mother's Day (UK)

_____
_____
_____
_____
_____

## QUESTION YOUR ACTIONS

During the frantic dance of every day, we often miss opportunities to discover what really matters to us. Right now write down three emotions you want to be true for your life - love, excitement, harmony and so on. Write down one action you can take each day this week to help you welcome your chosen emotions into your life.

# MARCH 7 – MARCH 13

*truth*

## 7 / MONDAY

Labour Day (WA)

## 8 / TUESDAY

International Women's Day

## 9 / WEDNESDAY ●

## NOTES

> "Truth, like gold, is to be obtained not by its growth,
> but by washing away from it all that is not gold."
>
> LEO TOLSTOY, RUSSIAN NOVELIST (1828-1910)

## 10 / THURSDAY

_____

_____

_____

_____

_____

_____

_____

_____

_____

_____

## 11 / FRIDAY

## 12 / SATURDAY

## 13 / SUNDAY

Daylight Savings Time Starts
(CAN, USA)

## WASH AWAY THE DIRT

Sometimes the truth we seek is within us already,
but covered with a film of dust. This week bring
back the shine to something you've had in your
life for a long time and may have taken for granted
- a relationship, a possession, or even a feeling.
Reconnect with why it is important to you and
cherish it anew.

# MARCH 14 – MARCH 20

*truth*

## 14 / MONDAY

Labour Day (VIC, TAS)
Commonwealth Day

## 15 / TUESDAY ☽

## 16 / WEDNESDAY

## NOTES

*"Between whom there is hearty truth, there is love."*

HENRY DAVID THOREAU, AMERICAN AUTHOR (1817-1862)

## 17 / THURSDAY

St Patrick's Day (NIR, ROI)

_____

_____

_____

_____

_____

_____

_____

_____

_____

_____

## 18 / FRIDAY

_____

_____

_____

_____

_____

_____

_____

_____

_____

_____

## 19 / SATURDAY

_____

_____

_____

_____

_____

## 20 / SUNDAY

Palm Sunday
Spring Equinox
Autumnal Equinox (AUS, NZ)

_____

_____

_____

### SPEAK ONE TRUE THING

Sometimes we avoid speaking the truth, either because it's painful to hear or painful to say. This week focus on *positive* truths. Identify one true, positive thing about someone you love - perhaps a lovely smile, or the way he or she handles tough situations - and tell him or her about it. The truth is easy when it's beautiful.

# MARCH 21 - MARCH 27

*truth*

## 21 / MONDAY ♈

_____
_____
_____
_____
_____
_____
_____
_____
_____
_____
_____
_____
_____

## 22 / TUESDAY

_____
_____
_____
_____
_____
_____
_____
_____
_____
_____
_____
_____
_____

## 23 / WEDNESDAY ○

Purim begins at sundown

_____
_____
_____
_____
_____
_____
_____
_____
_____
_____
_____
_____
_____

## NOTES

_____
_____
_____
_____

# "That man is best who sees the truth himself."

HESIOD, GREEK POET (750-650 BCE)

## 24 / THURSDAY
Maundy Thursday

_____

_____

_____

_____

_____

_____

_____

_____

_____

## 25 / FRIDAY
Good Friday

_____

_____

_____

_____

_____

_____

_____

_____

_____

## 26 / SATURDAY
Easter Saturday (AUS excluding WA and TAS)

_____

_____

_____

_____

## 27 / SUNDAY
Easter Sunday
British Summer Time begins

_____

_____

_____

_____

## DISCOVER INNER TRUTH

An essential aspect of self-awareness is knowing what's true within you. This week seek inner truth by listing seven attitudes or values (positive or negative) that have always been true for you. Each evening, light a candle to represent one item on your list – in doing so you are acknowledging the light of that truth within you.

# MARCH 28 – APRIL 3

*truth*

### 28 / MONDAY

Easter Monday

_____
_____
_____
_____
_____
_____
_____
_____
_____
_____
_____
_____

### 29 / TUESDAY

Easter Tuesday

_____
_____
_____
_____
_____
_____
_____
_____
_____
_____
_____
_____

### 30 / WEDNESDAY

_____
_____
_____
_____
_____
_____
_____
_____
_____
_____
_____
_____

## NOTES

_____
_____
_____
_____

> "Don't be satisfied with stories, how things have gone with others. Unfold your own myth."
>
> RUMI, PERSIAN POET AND SUFI MASTER (1207-1273)

## 31 / THURSDAY ☽

_____
_____
_____
_____
_____
_____
_____

## 1 / FRIDAY

April Fools' Day

_____
_____
_____
_____
_____
_____
_____

## 2 / SATURDAY

_____
_____
_____
_____

## 3 / SUNDAY

_____
_____
_____
_____

### WRITE YOUR OWN TRUTH

The truth is often easier to articulate when you write it down. Give yourself one hour this week to write your own story, just a paragraph of the facts about your life that brought you to where you are now. Then, consider the decisions that took you down this path and how those decisions reflect your personal truth.

# MARCH OVERVIEW

| M | TU | W | TH | F | SA | SU |
|---|----|----|----|----|----|----|
| 29 | 1 | 2 | 3 | 4 | 5 | 6 |
| 7 | 8 | 9 | 10 | 11 | 12 | 13 |
| 14 | 15 | 16 | 17 | 18 | 19 | 20 |
| 21 | 22 | 23 | 24 | 25 | 26 | 27 |
| 28 | 29 | 30 | 31 | 1 | 2 | 3 |

This month I am grateful for ...

_____

_____

_____

_____

_____

_____

_____

# Reflections on TRUTH

What did you learn about what's true for you this month?

_____

_____

_____

_____

_____

_____

In what ways did you make more informed decisions this month based on any truths
you discovered?

_____

_____

_____

_____

_____

_____

How do you plan to focus more on what's true for you in the future?

_____

_____

_____

_____

_____

_____

APRIL

# BEAUTY

Beauty is more than what we see - it surrounds us at every moment. It is in the laughter of a loved one, the changing of the seasons, the embrace of a friend. Like a peacock spreading his feathers to attract a mate, we must spread whatever beauty we can to attract even more beauty into our lives. We must also allow ourselves to be attracted to - and appreciative of - the beauty that is in everything. Paying proper attention to beauty may prove a challenge because we often take it for granted or are too busy to notice it. But if you allow yourself to slow down, to look around, to listen, to enjoy, you'll find that beauty surrounds you always.

### AFFIRMATION OF THE MONTH
I appreciate beauty in everything around me

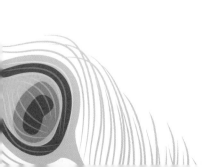

# APRIL 4 – APRIL 10

*beauty*

| 4 / MONDAY | 5 / TUESDAY | 6 / WEDNESDAY |
|------------|-------------|---------------|
|            |             |               |

NOTES

"There is no cosmetic for beauty like happiness."
MARGUERITE GARDINER, IRISH NOVELIST (1789-1849)

**7 / THURSDAY** ●

**8 / FRIDAY**

**9 / SATURDAY**

**10 / SUNDAY**

## SMILE AT YOURSELF

Sometimes we are critical of ourselves and we forget to see our own beauty. For one whole day this week, smile at yourself every time you see your reflection – in mirrors, windows, your computer screen. See how your face lights up when you smile, radiating the beauty within you.

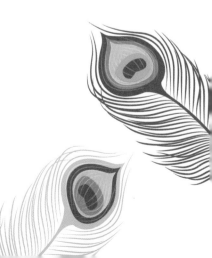

# APRIL 11 – APRIL 17

*beauty*

**11 / MONDAY**

**12 / TUESDAY**

**13 / WEDNESDAY**

NOTES

"Everything has beauty, but not everyone sees it."
CONFUCIUS, CHINESE PHILOSOPHER (551-479BCE)

**14 / THURSDAY** ☽

_____
_____
_____
_____
_____
_____
_____
_____
_____
_____
_____

**15 / FRIDAY**

_____
_____
_____
_____
_____
_____
_____
_____
_____
_____
_____

**16 / SATURDAY**

_____
_____
_____
_____
_____

**17 / SUNDAY**

_____
_____
_____
_____
_____
_____

### DISCOVER UNEXPECTED BEAUTY

It's easy to identify conventionally beautiful things – a blooming flower, a brilliant sunrise. This week concentrate on finding beauty in things that aren't classically beautiful – the dirty dish that recalls a delicious meal; the creases in your shoes that represent wonderful walks you've taken. Look for beauty everywhere.

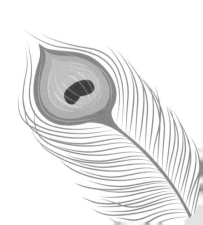

# APRIL 18 – APRIL 24

*beauty*

### 18 / MONDAY

_____
_____
_____
_____
_____
_____
_____
_____
_____
_____
_____
_____
_____

### 19 / TUESDAY

_____
_____
_____
_____
_____
_____
_____
_____
_____
_____
_____
_____
_____

### 20 / WEDNESDAY

_____
_____
_____
_____
_____
_____
_____
_____
_____
_____
_____
_____
_____

### NOTES

_____
_____
_____
_____

> *"Beauty is not in the face;*
> *beauty is a light in the heart."*
>
> KAHLIL GIBRAN, LEBANESE ARTIST AND WRITER (1883–1931)

## 21 / THURSDAY ♉

_____

_____

_____

_____

_____

_____

_____

_____

_____

## 22 / FRIDAY ○

Earth Day
Passover (Pesach) begins
at sundown

_____

_____

_____

_____

_____

_____

_____

_____

## 23 / SATURDAY

St George's Day

_____

_____

_____

_____

## 24 / SUNDAY

_____

_____

_____

_____

_____

## IDENTIFY HIDDEN BEAUTY

You've probably heard the saying: beauty comes from within. It's a cliché, but it's so true. So much of what makes others beautiful are the personality traits that shine through in their characteristics, words and actions. Every day this week identify two qualities that you have found beautiful in someone that day.

# APRIL 25 - MAY 1

*beauty*

### 25 / MONDAY

Anzac Day (AUS, NZ)

### 26 / TUESDAY

### 27 / WEDNESDAY

## NOTES

> *"Anyone who keeps the ability to see beauty never grows old."*
> FRANZ KAFKA, CZECH WRITER (1883-1924)

## 28 / THURSDAY

------------------
------------------
------------------
------------------
------------------
------------------
------------------
------------------
------------------

## 29 / FRIDAY

------------------
------------------
------------------
------------------
------------------
------------------
------------------
------------------

## 30 / SATURDAY ☾

Passover (Pesach) ends
at sundown

------------------
------------------
------------------

## 1 / SUNDAY

Beltane

------------------
------------------
------------------
------------------
------------------

### MARVEL LIKE A CHILD

Children marvel at the simplest things - the symmetry of marching ants, the shininess of dimples in an orange, the animal shapes of clouds in the sky - because their imaginations seek wonder and beauty in all things. This week give yourself permission to marvel like a child - look around for unexpected shapes, patterns and textures.

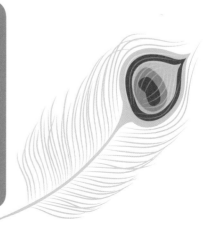

# APRIL OVERVIEW

| M | TU | W | TH | F | SA | SU |
|---|----|----|----|----|----|----|
| 28 | 29 | 30 | 31 | 1 | 2 | 3 |
| 4 | 5 | 6 | 7 | 8 | 9 | 10 |
| 11 | 12 | 13 | 14 | 15 | 16 | 17 |
| 18 | 19 | 20 | 21 | 22 | 23 | 24 |
| 25 | 26 | 27 | 28 | 29 | 30 | 1 |

This month I am grateful for ...

_____

_____

_____

_____

_____

_____

_____

_____

_____

# Reflections on BEAUTY

In what ways did you actively aim to find sources of beauty this month?

_____

_____

_____

_____

_____

How do you feel when you find beauty in even the most mundane things?

_____

_____

_____

_____

_____

In what ways can you bring a greater appreciation of beauty into your world?

_____

_____

_____

_____

_____

MAY

# SIMPLICITY

Over time we tend to layer up life – with activities, possessions and emotions, too, and we sometimes lose sight of how if feels to live simply, according to our innate needs and our innermost values. We start to believe that the busier we are and the more "stuff" we have around us, the more fulfilled we will be. But, actually, stripping back on commitments and clearing away clutter (mental and emotional, as well as physical) can make us feel lighter, liberated and more energized. This month is an opportunity to strip back the excess and embellishments of life and, like a single daisy standing tall in the grass, see how beauty and perfection lie in simplicity.

AFFIRMATION OF THE MONTH
*I seek simplicity in all things*

# MAY 2 – MAY 8

*simplicity*

## 2 / MONDAY

May Day Holiday (UK, ROI, NT)

## 3 / TUESDAY

## 4 / WEDNESDAY

## NOTES

"The art of being wise is the art of knowing what to overlook."

WILLIAM JAMES, AMERICAN PHILOSOPHER (1842-1910)

## 5 / THURSDAY

Cinco de Mayo
Ascension Day

## 6 / FRIDAY ●

## 7 / SATURDAY

## 8 / SUNDAY

Mother's Day (CAN, USA, AUS, NZ)

### SCHEDULE YOUR INBOX

Are you bombarded with messages and alerts? Each day this week put your phone and email on silent. Then, schedule four 30-minute slots for dealing with messages that have come in: Delete messages that are junk, flag those that require action, and respond immediately only to those that are urgent.

# MAY 9 – MAY 15

*simplicity*

## 9 / MONDAY

## 10 / TUESDAY

## 11 / WEDNESDAY

5TH period P.A.
cathup! Ask ?!
~~Go to Miss Haslam at lunch to get big~~
Go to miss Hill
at 8.am for
study leave
explanation.

Do Biology ~~mo~~
mock period
4 and Pick
up Physics
mock!

## NOTES

Go to Miss Haslam at lunch to get A3 sheet
of paper for exam calender/time table.

Go to Mr Smith at break bulletpoint the
key topics you missed to go over!

> *"Receive with simplicity everything that happens to you."*
>
> RASHI, FRENCH RABBI (1040-1105)

Figure out when
Heal revision sessions
are !

## 12 / THURSDAY

Aden lunchtime shoot!

~~Go to.~~
Collect all
workbook
for every
~~sketch b~~
Subject !!!
'For revision !

Collect condenced
revision sheet
for biology from
Miss Champion!

Pay for prom with letter!

## 13 / FRIDAY ☽

Physics revision
after school!

Download
BBC Bitesize
app on phone!

## 14 / SATURDAY

Buddha's birthday
(in some countries)

## 15 / SUNDAY

Pentecost (Whit Sunday)

## SIMPLIFY YOUR INTERACTIONS

We complicate interactions with others by looking for subtext or hidden meaning - often when there is none. This week cultivate an attitude of simple acceptance in your interactions. Greet a kind word with a simple "thank you", or a new task from your boss with "I'm on it!"

Figure out what is happening tomorrow!

| 16 / MONDAY | 17 / TUESDAY | 18 / WEDNESDAY |
|---|---|---|
| | ✓ | ✓ |
| | Biology revision | Chemistry revision |
| | a.m. B1 Core | a.m. C1 Core |
| | S304, S405, S310. | S 304, S405, S302 |
| | | |
| | Biology unit 1 | English Literatu |
| | Higher 13:30 p.m | p.m. revision |
| | 60 mins GCSE | 318, 316, 308, 312. |
| | | Inspector Calls & |
| | | OFMice and men, Plan. |

## NOTES

Complete all Clements course work by
next week use old tick list and print
every thing out and stick it in course work
folder!

> *"I am beginning to learn that it is the sweet, simple things of life which are the real ones after all."*
>
> LAURA INGALLS WILDER, AMERICAN WRITER (1867-1957)

## 19 / THURSDAY

✓

Chemistry unit
1 Higher 09:00
a.m. 60 minutes.

## 20 / FRIDAY

## 21 / SATURDAY ○ Ⅱ

Complete all
P.A. Dev course
work using
new to do list
also make final

## 22 / SUNDAY

result props and
set swor. print
everything out
and put in final
folder with
other coursework.

### FIND A SWEET, SIMPLE ACT

Moments of sweetness are often without frills –
but these moments can pass so quickly that we
don't stop to appreciate them. This week identify
one simple act that makes you happy – your
morning coffee, holding hands with your child,
a hug from your partner – and make an effort
to appreciate its simple beauty.

# MAY 23 - MAY 29

*simplicity*

## 23 / MONDAY

Victoria Day (CAN, except NS, NU, QC)

Maths p.m. ✓
revision, F307
Mr J. Graham.

English literature ✓
unit 1 Higher a.m.
90 minutes 09:00

## 24 / TUESDAY

Geography a.m. ✓
Mr P Smith revision
F526 Unit 1 Higher.

Geography ~~unit~~ ✓
Higher theory
105 minutes p.m.
13:30 GCSE

## 25 / WEDNESDAY

Physics a.m. ✓
P1 Core S304,
S405, S404,
Single science.

Physics unit 1
Higher 60 minutes
13:30 p.m. GCSE

## NOTES

*"Beware the barrenness of a busy life."*

SOCRATES, GREEK PHILOSOPHER (469-399BCE)

**26 / THURSDAY**   **27 / FRIDAY**   **28 / SATURDAY**

✓ English Literature   ✓ English literature
p.m. revision         unit 2 Higher
318, 316, 308, 312.   75 minutes a.m.
Poetry, comparing.    09:00 GCSE
                      Poetry ↗

Maths Non Calculator                    **29 / SUNDAY** ☾
105 minutes Higher
09:00 a.m.

### CHERISH THE ESSENTIALS

One day this week clear your diary of all non-essentials. Be ruthless - postpone unimportant meetings and cancel your errands. On your chosen day fully engage with life's essentials - bathing, eating, sleeping, loving - and appreciate how enriching it is to fully experience each act.

# MAY OVERVIEW

| M | TU | W | TH | F | SA | SU |
|---|----|----|----|----|----|----|
| 25 | 26 | 27 | 28 | 29 | 30 | 1 |
| 2 | 3 | 4 | 5 | 6 | 7 | 8 |
| 9 | 10 | 11 | 12 | 13 | 14 | 15 |
| 16 | 17 | 18 | 19 | 20 | 21 | 22 |
| 23 | 24 | 25 | 26 | 27 | 28 | 29 |
| 30 | 31 | 1 | 2 | 3 | 4 | 5 |

This month I am grateful for ...

_____

_____

_____

_____

_____

_____

# Reflections on SIMPLICITY

In what ways did you choose to simplify your life this month?

_____

_____

_____

_____

_____

How did you feel when you had simplified areas and activities in your life?

_____

_____

_____

_____

_____

Are there any techniques you'll continue to use beyond the end of this month?
What further practices can you put in place to make life simpler?

_____

_____

_____

_____

_____

JUNE

# KINDNESS

Kindness offers a deep and powerful way to connect with others and with yourself. When you act and speak kindly, your heart fills with love, your soul with clarity, and your thoughts with peace. It's wonderfully contagious, too: one kind act can have a ripple effect that creates a whole community connected by compassion and love. Make this month a time to give the people and commitments in your life some loving attention. Every day offers opportunities to show compassion and empathy towards others, to brighten someone else's world, to go easy on yourself. The activities for June will help you to tune in to the kindness you may have been taking for granted in your life, and to remember to be kind to yourself as well as others.

## AFFIRMATION OF THE MONTH

I commit myself to giving and receiving kindness

# MAY 30 – JUNE 5

*kindness*

## 30 / MONDAY

Spring Bank Holiday (UK)
Memorial Day (USA)

## 31 / TUESDAY

## 1 / WEDNESDAY

## NOTES

"Wherever there is a human being, there is
an opportunity for a kindness."

SENECA, ROMAN PHILOSOPHER (4BCE–65CE)

## 2 / THURSDAY

_____
_____
_____
_____
_____
_____
_____
_____
_____
_____

## 3 / FRIDAY

_____
_____
_____
_____
_____
_____
_____
_____
_____
_____

## 4 / SATURDAY

_____
_____
_____
_____

## 5 / SUNDAY ●

_____
_____
_____
_____
_____

### SHARE A SMILE

Every interaction you have with another person is
an opportunity to be kind. Simply acknowledging
someone with a smile can make that person feel
valued and joyful. Choose one day this week to
spread kindness by smiling, from your heart, at
every person you encounter. And enjoy every
smile that radiates back at you.

# JUNE 6 – JUNE 12

*kindness*

## 6 / MONDAY

June Bank Holiday (ROI)
Queen's birthday celebrated (NZ)
Ramadan begins at sundown

English language ✓
p.m. revision, 318,
316, 312, 322,
Unseen extracts.

## 7 / TUESDAY

✓

Maths p.m. revision
F310, F307, F304,
Mr J. Graham.

Geography a.m.
revision Mr P. Smith
F526 Unit 2 Higher.  } →

English language
unit 2 Higher
175 minutes
a.m. 09:00

## 8 / WEDNESDAY

✓

Geography
Higher theory
75 minutes
13:30 p.m. GCSE

## NOTES

> *"Kind words can be short and easy to speak, but their echoes are truly endless."*
>
> MOTHER TERESA, CATHOLIC MISSIONARY (1910-1997)

## 9 / THURSDAY

Biology p.m. ✓
revision. B2
Double additional,
S310, S308, S304,
S306, S302, Science.

Maths Calculator
Higher 105 minutes
09:00 a.m.

## 10 / FRIDAY

Biology unit 2 ✓
Higher 60 minutes
09:00 a.m.

## 11 / SATURDAY

## 12 / SUNDAY ☽

### SEND OUT POSITIVITY

Having someone speak to or about you with kindness brings about wonderful, warm feelings. Share those feelings in three ways this week: leave a kind note on a colleague's desk, a kind comment on a blog or website you enjoy reading, and a kind message on a loved one's voicemail.

# JUNE 13 – JUNE 19

*kindness*

## 13 / MONDAY

Queen's birthday celebrated
(AUS excluding WA)

Physics ✓
~~Chemistry~~ p.m.
revision C2
additional, Science
Mr Goddard
period 4/5
S302, S310,
S308, S304.

## 14 / TUESDAY

## 15 / WEDNESDAY

Chemistry unit 2
Higher 60 minutes
13:30 p.m.
Chemistry
~~Physics~~ a.m.
revision P2,
additional Science
Mr Sullivan
Period 2/3,
S404, S310,
S312, S306,

## NOTES

> *"You, yourself, as much as anybody in the entire universe, deserve your love and affection."*
>
> GAUTAMA BUDDHA (*C.* 480–400BCE)

## 16 / THURSDAY

## 17 / FRIDAY

Physics unit 2
Higher 60 minutes
09:00 p.a.m.

## 18 / SATURDAY

Seven Oacks
festival D&B
Performance
Competition
"Fight over fushia"

## 19 / SUNDAY

Father's Day (UK, CAN, USA)

# JUNE 20 - JUNE 26

*kindness*

## 20 / MONDAY ○

Summer Solstice
Winter Solstice (AUS, NZ)

## 21 / TUESDAY

## 22 / WEDNESDAY ♋

Thinking & ✓
Reasoning p.m.
revision, Lecture
Theatre paper 1
S305 paper 2 S303.

## NOTES

> "Three things ... are important: the first is to be kind; the second is to be kind; and the third is to be kind."

HENRY JAMES, AMERICAN-BRITISH WRITER (1843-1916)

**23 / THURSDAY**

Thinking & Reasoning
skills written
60 minutes
09:00 a.m.

**24 / FRIDAY**

**25 / SATURDAY**

**26 / SUNDAY**

## BE A KINDNESS GENIE

Unexpected kindness is like a little bit of magic.
This week commit three random acts of kindness,
such as: pay for someone behind you in a queue,
make an anonymous donation, write a thank-you note
to your postman, do someone else's household chore
or bake a cake for your neighbour.

# JUNE 27 - JULY 3
*kindness*

Thinking & Reasoning
skills case study
60 minutes
09:00 a.m
Last GCSE :)!

PROM
IS
TODAY
:)

6ᵀᴴ form taster
day!

## NOTES

*"No act of kindness, no matter how small, is ever wasted."*

AESOP, ANCIENT GREEK STORYTELLER (620–564 BCE)

**30 / THURSDAY**

Today
NCS
starts ☺

**1 / FRIDAY**

Canada Day

**2 / SATURDAY**

**3 / SUNDAY**

## WRITE A NOTE

The smallest acts, thoughtfully crafted, are often the kindest. This week write a letter of love to someone who is close to you. Be specific in how you express gratitude for the fact that that person is in your life; give examples of the ways in which you're particularly grateful for him or her.

# JUNE OVERVIEW

| M | TU | W | TH | F | SA | SU |
|---|---|---|---|---|---|---|
| 30 | 31 | 1 | 2 | 3 | 4 | 5 |
| 6 | 7 | 8 | 9 | 10 | 11 | 12 |
| 13 | 14 | 15 | 16 | 17 | 18 | 19 |
| 20 | 21 | 22 | 23 | 24 | 25 | 26 |
| 27 | 28 | 29 | 30 | 1 | 2 | 3 |

This month I am grateful for ...

_____

_____

_____

_____

_____

_____

_____

_____

# Reflections on KINDNESS

In what specific ways have you given or received kindness this month?

_____

_____

_____

_____

_____

How does it make you feel when you act purely out of kindness?
What feelings do you hope to evoke in others through your actions?

_____

_____

_____

_____

_____

How can you nurture more kindness in your life?

_____

_____

_____

_____

_____

_____

JULY

# MINDFULNESS

Although its origins lie in Buddhist meditation, mindfulness - the act of being fully present in the moment - is accessible to us all. When we focus completely on one thing - a thought, emotion, object or action - our sensory perception increases and, like the opening of a lotus flower, we become open to all the possibilities of our experience. Full immersion in the present also means we can't worry about what's happened in the past or agonize about what might happen in the future. Stress falls away and the present becomes a more joyful and fulfilling place. This month's activities will help you practise being mindful of every moment. Distractions abound, so it's not always easy, but the more you practise, the more naturally mindfulness will come.

AFFIRMATION OF THE MONTH
*I am able to focus mindfully
on one thing at a time*

# JULY 4 – JULY 10
*mindfulness*

## 4 / MONDAY ●

Independence Day (USA)

_____
_____
_____
_____
_____
_____
_____
_____
_____
_____

## 5 / TUESDAY

Eid-al-Fitr (end of Ramadan)
begins at sundown

_____
_____
_____
_____
_____
_____
_____
_____
_____
_____

## 6 / WEDNESDAY

_____
_____
_____
_____
_____
_____
_____
_____
_____
_____

## NOTES

_____
_____
_____
_____

> "With the past, I have nothing to do;
> nor with the future. I live now."
>
> RALPH WALDO EMERSON, AMERICAN ESSAYIST (1803-1882)

## 7 / THURSDAY

## 8 / FRIDAY

## 9 / SATURDAY

### 10 / SUNDAY

MY
BIRTHDAY
!☺ SWEET
16 TH ♡

## USE YOUR SENSES

Our senses provide a wonderful way to connect us to the present. Match each weekday with one sense – perhaps, sight on Monday; hearing on Tuesday and so on. Whenever you become distracted from the present, tune in to that sense and focus on what you're experiencing, immersing yourself in that moment.

# JULY 11 – JULY 17
*mindfulness*

**11 / MONDAY**

**12 / TUESDAY** ☽

Orangemen's Day (NI)

**13 / WEDNESDAY**

NOTES

> "The best thing about the future is that it comes one day at a time."
>
> ABRAHAM LINCOLN, AMERICAN PRESIDENT (1809-1865)

## 14 / THURSDAY

Bastille Day

_____

_____

_____

_____

_____

_____

_____

_____

_____

_____

_____

## 15 / FRIDAY

_____

_____

_____

_____

_____

_____

_____

_____

_____

_____

_____

## 16 / SATURDAY

_____

_____

_____

_____

## 17 / SUNDAY

_____

_____

_____

_____

_____

_____

_____

### TAKE A FREE DAY

Planning is an important way to schedule your time. But if it leads you to worry so much about what's to come that you don't enjoy what's happening now, it's a barrier to mindfulness. Make one day this week a "free" day: no to-do list; no calendar. Enjoy the natural rhythm of the day, as it comes.

# JULY 18 – JULY 24 *mindfulness*

**18 / MONDAY**

**19 / TUESDAY** ○

**20 / WEDNESDAY**

_____
_____
_____
_____
_____
_____
_____
_____
_____
_____
_____
_____
_____

## NOTES

_____
_____
_____
_____

# "Nothing is worth more than this day."

JOHANN WOLFGANG VON GOETHE, GERMAN WRITER (1749-1832)

**21 / THURSDAY**

**22 / FRIDAY**

**23 / SATURDAY** ♌

_____

_____

_____

_____

_____

_____

_____

_____

_____

_____

_____

_____

_____

_____

_____

_____

_____

**24 / SUNDAY**

_____

_____

_____

_____

_____

_____

_____

_____

_____

_____

_____

_____

_____

_____

_____

## LIST THE AMAZING

When you think about it, today is the only day. It's not over (like days past) and it's not unknown (like days to come). Today matters most, so take note of what's wonderful about it. At the end of every day this week, make a list of that day's top ten highlights.

# JULY 25 – JULY 31
*mindfulness*

25 / MONDAY                 26 / TUESDAY                 27 / WEDNESDAY ☾

NOTES

> "All that we are is the result of what we have thought. The mind is everything. What we think we become."
>
> GAUTAMA BUDDHA (C. 480–400BCE)

## 28 / THURSDAY

_____

_____

_____

_____

_____

_____

_____

_____

_____

_____

## 29 / FRIDAY

_____

_____

_____

_____

_____

_____

_____

_____

_____

_____

## 30 / SATURDAY

_____

_____

_____

_____

## 31 / SUNDAY

_____

_____

_____

_____

_____

_____

### USE THE "TAP" METHOD

Your thoughts have the power to direct your life in positive ways. This week use the TAP method to pay attention to your thoughts about yourself. When you feel a self-judgment creeping in, ask yourself: Is this thought **T**rue? Is it **A**dding value? Is it **P**ositive? If the thought doesn't meet those three criteria, let it go.

# JULY OVERVIEW

| M | TU | W | TH | F | SA | SU |
|---|----|----|----|----|----|----|
| 27 | 28 | 29 | 30 | 1 | 2 | 3 |
| 4 | 5 | 6 | 7 | 8 | 9 | 10 |
| 11 | 12 | 13 | 14 | 15 | 16 | 17 |
| 18 | 19 | 20 | 21 | 22 | 23 | 24 |
| 25 | 26 | 27 | 28 | 29 | 30 | 31 |

This month I am grateful for ...

_____

_____

_____

_____

_____

_____

_____

_____

# Reflections on MINDFULNESS

What circumstances this month made mindfulness easy? When was it most difficult?

_____

_____

_____

_____

_____

How did you feel when you were able to remain in the present moment rather than worrying about the past and the future?

_____

_____

_____

_____

_____

What techniques could help you bring more mindfulness into your life in the future?

_____

_____

_____

_____

_____

_____

AUGUST

# GRATITUDE

Being thankful for all that we have in our lives (rather than focusing on what we don't have) makes it almost impossible to be unhappy or negative. Our world becomes less a place of craving or wanting, and more a place of happy satisfaction, where what we have is enough. The power of gratitude is like the energy that lies within the smallest seed. Plant that seed and, even when life is hard and it feels as though there is little to be grateful for, nurture it with moments of thankfulness. Eventually the seed will bear great fruit that can sweeten even the darkest days. The activities this month encourage you to choose gratitude and help you to find something to be thankful for in every moment of your life.

## AFFIRMATION OF THE MONTH

*I choose to be grateful for all I have and all I am*

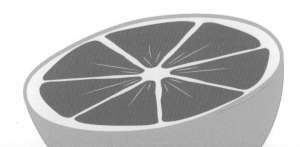

# AUGUST 1 - AUGUST 7

*gratitude*

### 1 / MONDAY

Lughnasadh (Lammas)
August Bank Holiday (RI)

### 2 / TUESDAY ●

### 3 / WEDNESDAY

### NOTES

> "Gratitude is not only the greatest of virtues, but the parent of all others."
>
> MARCUS TULLIUS CICERO, ROMAN PHILOSOPHER (107-44BCE)

**4 / THURSDAY**

_____
_____
_____
_____
_____
_____

_____
_____
_____
_____

**5 / FRIDAY**

_____
_____
_____
_____
_____
_____

_____
_____
_____
_____

**6 / SATURDAY**

_____
_____
_____
_____

**7 / SUNDAY**

_____
_____
_____
_____
_____

### EXTEND YOUR VIRTUE

Gratitude lays the foundation for other positive behaviours - kindness, humility and compassion, for example. Each evening this week note one reason the day has given you to be grateful. How can your gratitude translate to another virtuous behaviour? For example, gratitude for your healthy children might give you patience, and so on.

# AUGUST 8 - AUGUST 14

*gratitude*

**8 / MONDAY**

**9 / TUESDAY**

**10 / WEDNESDAY** ☽

**NOTES**

*"Do not spoil what you have by desiring what you have not."*
EPICTETUS, GREEK PHILOSOPHER (55-135 CE)

## 11 / THURSDAY

_____
_____
_____
_____
_____
_____
_____
_____
_____
_____

## 12 / FRIDAY

_____
_____
_____
_____
_____
_____
_____
_____
_____
_____

## 13 / SATURDAY

_____
_____
_____
_____

## 14 / SUNDAY

_____
_____
_____
_____
_____

## LIST YOUR FAVOURITES

Habitually wanting more - time, energy, happiness, money - means missing opportunities to enjoy what we already have. At the start of the week, make a list of your favourite things - a hobby, a friend, your health, the view from your kitchen - and put it where you can see it. Whenever you wish you had more, glance over, smile and be thankful.

# AUGUST 15 - AUGUST 21

*gratitude*

### 15 / MONDAY

### 16 / TUESDAY

### 17 / WEDNESDAY

## NOTES

*"Some people grumble that roses have thorns;
I am grateful that thorns have roses."*

ALPHONSE KARR, FRENCH JOURNALIST (1808-1890)

18 / THURSDAY ○

19 / FRIDAY

20 / SATURDAY

_____

_____

_____

_____

_____

_____

_____

21 / SUNDAY

_____

_____

_____

## FIND THE BRIGHT SIDE

When a situation seems gloomy, it's sometimes easy to focus on the gloom. This week pinpoint one thing that's less than ideal in your life - maybe it's your job, relationship or financial situation - and ask yourself: *What is going right in this situation?* Feeling grateful for the rose among the thorns provides colour in an otherwise grey situation.

# AUGUST 22 - AUGUST 28

*gratitude*

**22 / MONDAY**

**23 / TUESDAY**

**24 / WEDNESDAY** ♍

NOTES

> "Each of us has cause to think with deep gratitude of those who have lighted the flame within us."
>
> ALBERT SCHWEITZER, GERMAN THEOLOGIAN (1875-1965)

## 25 / THURSDAY ☾

_____
_____
_____
_____
_____
_____
_____
_____
_____
_____

## 26 / FRIDAY

_____
_____
_____
_____
_____
_____
_____
_____
_____
_____

## 27 / SATURDAY

_____
_____
_____
_____

## 28 / SUNDAY

_____
_____
_____
_____
_____
_____
_____

## SHOWING GRATITUDE

It's so important to be grateful for the people who support you. Identify someone you're thankful for and choose one day this week to celebrate that person in style. If he or she is nearby, meet for dinner or have a party; if far away, send a card, Champagne, a cake or a balloon.

# AUGUST OVERVIEW

| M | TU | W | TH | F | SA | SU |
|---|----|----|----|----|----|----|
| 1 | 2 | 3 | 4 | 5 | 6 | 7 |
| 8 | 9 | 10 | 11 | 12 | 13 | 14 |
| 15 | 16 | 17 | 18 | 19 | 20 | 21 |
| 22 | 23 | 24 | 25 | 26 | 27 | 28 |
| 29 | 30 | 31 | 1 | 2 | 3 | 4 |

This month I am grateful for ...

_____

_____

_____

_____

_____

_____

_____

_____

# Reflections on GRATITUDE

In what ways did you cultivate an attitude of gratitude this month?
What are you most grateful for right now?

_____

_____

_____

_____

_____

_____

In what ways do you feel more positive about yourself and your life when you actively
aim to be thankful?

_____

_____

_____

_____

_____

_____

How will you keep gratitude a priority in your life in the future?

_____

_____

_____

_____

_____

# WISDOM

We often think of wisdom as something that comes with age, but intelligence, common sense, experience and knowledge (the ingredients that make us wise) can arrive at any point in our lives - as long as we are attentive to what we see, hear, think and do. Like a tree, wisdom takes time to take root, to grow and to bear fruit. Regardless of where you are in your life, you've already planted the roots of your wisdom and this month's activities will help you to recognize and appreciate the wisdom you already possess. They will also encourage you to explore new ways to gather wisdom from your experiences and from those around you.

## AFFIRMATION OF THE MONTH

*I seek to draw wisdom from everything and everyone around me*

# AUGUST 29 - SEPTEMBER 4

*wisdom*

## 29 / MONDAY

Summer Bank Holiday (UK)

## 30 / TUESDAY

## 31 / WEDNESDAY

## NOTES

*"Wisdom is not wisdom when it is derived from books alone."*

HORACE, ROMAN POET (65-8BCE)

## 1 / THURSDAY ●

## 2 / FRIDAY

## 3 / SATURDAY

## 4 / SUNDAY

Father's Day (AUS, NZ)

### PRACTISE WHAT YOU LEARN

Books can give us knowledge, but it's experience that typically brings wisdom. This week, identify an activity you've always wanted to try. Like the sound of climbing? Find a climbing centre and give it a go. Always wanted to try cooking with lentils? Look up a recipe and cook it! Ideas + action = wisdom!

# SEPTEMBER 5 – SEPTEMBER 11

*wisdom*

## 5 / MONDAY

Labor Day (CAN, USA)

## 6 / TUESDAY

## 7 / WEDNESDAY

## NOTES

> *"Knowing yourself is the beginning of all wisdom."*
> ARISTOTLE, GREEK PHILOSOPHER (384-322BCE)

## 8 / THURSDAY

_____
_____
_____
_____
_____
_____
_____
_____
_____
_____
_____

## 9 / FRIDAY ☽

_____
_____
_____
_____
_____
_____
_____
_____
_____
_____
_____

## 10 / SATURDAY

_____
_____
_____
_____

## 11 / SUNDAY

_____
_____
_____
_____
_____
_____

### KNOW YOURSELF

The wisest people are those with the greatest self-awareness. At the end of every day this week, think about one action, response or decision you made that day. What motivated you? What does your action tell you about yourself? Would you advise for or against this action in the future? Why?

# SEPTEMBER 12 - SEPTEMBER 18

*wisdom*

**12 / MONDAY**

**13 / TUESDAY**

**14 / WEDNESDAY**

**NOTES**

> *"Anyone who stops learning is old, whether at twenty or eighty."*
>
> HENRY FORD, AMERICAN INDUSTRIALIST (1863-1947)

## 15 / THURSDAY

_____
_____
_____
_____
_____
_____
_____
_____
_____
_____
_____

## 16 / FRIDAY ○

_____
_____
_____
_____
_____
_____
_____
_____
_____
_____
_____

## 17 / SATURDAY

_____
_____
_____
_____

## 18 / SUNDAY

_____
_____
_____
_____
_____
_____
_____

### LEARN FROM OTHERS

We can gain great insights by learning from others.
Be alert this week to someone doing something
or responding differently from the way you would.
Instead of feeling agitated by differences, consider
them with an open mind and think about how you
could combine approaches perhaps for the best
outcome of all.

# SEPTEMBER 19 – SEPTEMBER 25

*wisdom*

### 19 / MONDAY

### 20 / TUESDAY

### 21 / WEDNESDAY

International Day of Peace

## NOTES

> *"Patience is the companion of wisdom."*
>
> ST. AUGUSTINE, CHRISTIAN THEOLOGIAN (354–430)

## 22 / THURSDAY

Autumn Equinox (UK, ROI, USA, CAN)
Spring Equinox (AUS, NZ)

## 23 / FRIDAY ☾

## 24 / SATURDAY ♎

## 25 / SUNDAY

## CULTIVATE PATIENCE

Patience and wisdom go hand in hand, because wisdom takes time. Cultivate patience this week by sitting in silence for 10 to 15 minutes every day. If it suits you, try meditation; if not, simply sit still and count your breaths in and out, bringing your attention back to your breath if it wanders.

# SEPTEMBER 26 - OCTOBER 2

*wisdom*

### 26 / MONDAY
Queen's birthday celebrated (WA)

### 27 / TUESDAY

### 28 / WEDNESDAY

## NOTES

> *"It is unwise to be too sure of one's own wisdom."*
>
> MAHATMA GANDHI, INDIAN LEADER (1869-1948)

## 29 / THURSDAY

_____

_____

_____

_____

_____

_____

_____

_____

_____

## 30 / FRIDAY

_____

_____

_____

_____

_____

_____

_____

_____

_____

## 1 / SATURDAY ●

Al-Hijra / Muharram (Islamic New Year) begins at sundown
Black History Month begins (UK)

_____

_____

## 2 / SUNDAY

Rosh Hashanah (Jewish New Year) begins at sundown

_____

_____

_____

## QUESTION YOUR WISDOM

Those who are truly wise don't make assumptions. This week write down three things you think you know for sure - such as how your partner will react to a certain situation or how you'll feel during a meeting. Now look more closely and ponder: *Am I certain these things are true? How might I view them differently?*

# SEPTEMBER OVERVIEW

| M | TU | W | TH | F | SA | SU |
|---|---|---|---|---|---|---|
| 29 | 30 | 31 | 1 | 2 | 3 | 4 |
| 5 | 6 | 7 | 8 | 9 | 10 | 11 |
| 12 | 13 | 14 | 15 | 16 | 17 | 18 |
| 19 | 20 | 21 | 22 | 23 | 24 | 25 |
| 26 | 27 | 28 | 29 | 30 | 1 | 2 |

This month I am grateful for ...

_____

_____

_____

_____

_____

_____

_____

# Reflections on WISDOM

What wisdom did you gain this month and how did you gain it?

_____

_____

_____

_____

_____

How did it make you feel to share wisdom with others in a positive way?

_____

_____

_____

_____

_____

How can you become more open-minded about gaining wisdom in the future?

_____

_____

_____

_____

_____

_____

# OCTOBER

# COURAGE

When we think of courage, we often think of immense strength or bravery - warriors in battle, mothers protecting their young, heroes who stand up to their enemies - but it also takes courage to face up to emotions, situations or thoughts that worry or scare us. Courage is about seeing a mountain before you and choosing to begin the climb, having the strength to keep going even when it's difficult, and believing you can take another step even when you want to stop. Courage is about choosing what's right over what's easy, putting others before yourself, facing fear, and welcoming difficult emotions. The activities this month invite you to acknowledge and celebrate the courage within you, and to recognize how incredibly brave you are just by being you.

### AFFIRMATION OF THE MONTH

*I celebrate the courage that lies within me*

# OCTOBER 3 – OCTOBER 9

*courage*

### 3 / MONDAY

Labour Day (ACT, NSW, SA, QLD)

### 4 / TUESDAY

### 5 / WEDNESDAY

NOTES

*"Courage is resistance to fear, mastery of fear — not absence of fear."*

MARK TWAIN, AMERICAN AUTHOR (1835-1910)

## 6 / THURSDAY

## 7 / FRIDAY

## 8 / SATURDAY

## 9 / SUNDAY ☽

## WELCOME YOUR FEARS

Your fears are opportunities for you to celebrate your bravery. Pick one day this week to do something you've been afraid to do - ask for a pay rise, go skydiving, say "I love you", wear a bold new style - and do it! Once you've conquered one fear - no matter how small - you'll feel filled with courage.

# OCTOBER 10 – OCTOBER 16

*courage*

## 10 / MONDAY

Thanksgiving Day (CAN)
Columbus Day

## 11 / TUESDAY

Yom Kippur (Day of Atonement)
begins at sundown

## 12 / WEDNESDAY

## NOTES

"I can shake off everything as I write; my sorrows disappear, my courage is reborn."

ANNE FRANK, GERMAN DIARIST (1929-1945)

## 13 / THURSDAY

_____
_____
_____
_____
_____
_____
_____
_____
_____
_____
_____

## 14 / FRIDAY

_____
_____
_____
_____
_____
_____
_____
_____
_____
_____
_____

## 15 / SATURDAY

_____
_____
_____
_____
_____

## 16 / SUNDAY ○

_____
_____
_____
_____
_____

### WRITE IT DOWN

The act of writing is a courageous one. When you put words on paper or screen, your thoughts become real. Spend 30 minutes this week writing about something you fear – you don't have to share it with anyone if you don't want to. In giving your fear a voice, you breathe life into the courage you need to conquer it.

# OCTOBER 17 - OCTOBER 23

*courage*

**17 / MONDAY**

**18 / TUESDAY**

**19 / WEDNESDAY**

NOTES

"You don't have to see the whole staircase
– just take the first step."
MARTIN LUTHER KING, JR., AMERICAN ACTIVIST (1929-1968)

20 / THURSDAY

21 / FRIDAY

22 / SATURDAY ☾

_____

_____

_____

_____

_____

_____

23 / SUNDAY

_____

_____

_____

_____

## TAKE ONE STEP

Courage can begin with one step in the right direction. One evening this week, tackle a task you've been putting off for a while by taking one small step towards accomplishing it (even if that step is simply making a list of what you need to do).

# OCTOBER 24 – OCTOBER 30
*courage*

**24 / MONDAY** ♏

Labour Day (NZ)

**25 / TUESDAY**

**26 / WEDNESDAY**

NOTES

"Success is not final, failure is not fatal: it is the courage to continue that counts."

WINSTON CHURCHILL, BRITISH PRIME MINISTER (1874–1965)

## 27 / THURSDAY

_____
_____
_____
_____
_____
_____
_____
_____
_____
_____

## 28 / FRIDAY

_____
_____
_____
_____
_____
_____
_____
_____
_____
_____

## 29 / SATURDAY

_____
_____
_____
_____

## 30 / SUNDAY ●

British Summer Time ends
Diwali (Festival of Lights)

_____
_____
_____

### RECOGNIZE YOUR STRENGTH

What we might think of as "failure" can, in fact, lead us to accomplish wonderful things. Think of something you feel you've failed at and consider instead how you might have actually shown courage in the situation and what positive effects – for your life or the lives of others – you might have created.

# OCTOBER OVERVIEW

| M | TU | W | TH | F | SA | SU |
|---|---|---|---|---|---|---|
| 26 | 27 | 28 | 29 | 30 | 1 | 2 |
| 3 | 4 | 5 | 6 | 7 | 8 | 9 |
| 10 | 11 | 12 | 13 | 14 | 15 | 16 |
| 17 | 18 | 19 | 20 | 21 | 22 | 23 |
| 24 | 25 | 26 | 27 | 28 | 29 | 30 |
| 31 | 1 | 2 | 3 | 4 | 5 | 6 |

This month I am grateful for ...

_____

_____

_____

_____

_____

_____

_____

# Reflections on COURAGE

In what ways have you tapped into your reserves of courage this month?

_____

_____

_____

_____

_____

How did overcoming your fears, however small, make you feel?

_____

_____

_____

_____

_____

How do you think you can become more courageous in the future?
What would you like to overcome?

_____

_____

_____

_____

_____

# NOVEMBER

# CURIOSITY

Talk to a child for more than a minute and you'll find boundless curiosity: *Why? How? What for?* As adults we tend to push aside this questioning nature to focus on things we already understand (like our jobs) or things we have to get done. But, there is always so much more to learn about the world around us! The urge to discover can permeate all aspects of life - work, relationships, the self. The more interested we are, the more tuned in to our lives we become. Cultivating curiosity can expose us not only to new information, but also to new ways of thinking, which can positively impact our lives on a day-to-day basis. This month's activities will help you to imagine yourself as a tiny part of a gigantic universe and to open your heart and mind to exploring all that you do not yet know.

## AFFIRMATION OF THE MONTH

*I am passionately curious about my world*

# OCTOBER 31 – NOVEMBER 6

*curiosity*

## 31 / MONDAY

October Bank Holiday (ROI)
Halloween
Samhain

## 1 / TUESDAY

All Saints' Day

## 2 / WEDNESDAY

All Souls' Day

## NOTES

> *"Life was meant to be lived, and curiosity must be kept alive."*
> ELEANOR ROOSEVELT, AMERICAN POLITICIAN (1884-1962)

## 3 / THURSDAY

_____
_____
_____
_____
_____
_____
_____
_____
_____
_____

## 4 / FRIDAY

_____
_____
_____
_____
_____
_____
_____
_____
_____
_____

## 5 / SATURDAY

_____
_____
_____
_____

## 6 / SUNDAY

_____
_____
_____
_____
_____

## ASK NEW QUESTIONS

Children tend to be unabashed about asking questions to find out about others; adults often get anxious about asking too much. Meet a friend with the aim of discovering something about them you didn't already know - a great passion, an interesting heritage, the name of their first love. Your curiosity will strengthen the bond between you.

# NOVEMBER 7 – NOVEMBER 13

*curiosity*

| 7 / MONDAY ☽ | 8 / TUESDAY | 9 / WEDNESDAY |
|---|---|---|
| | | |

NOTES

*"The mind is not a vessel to be filled,
but a fire to be kindled."*

PLUTARCH, GREEK HISTORIAN (C. 46-120CE)

## 10 / THURSDAY

_____

_____

_____

_____

_____

_____

_____

_____

_____

_____

## 11 / FRIDAY

Remembrance Day (CAN)
Veterans Day (USA)

_____

_____

_____

_____

_____

_____

_____

_____

_____

## 12 / SATURDAY

_____

_____

_____

_____

## 13 / SUNDAY

Remembrance Sunday

_____

_____

_____

_____

_____

### STIMULATE YOUR MIND

It's tempting to think of curiosity as an opportunity
to stock up on facts, but real curiosity is driven by
passion for deep understanding. Set aside an hour
or two this week to research a topic that inspires you
– new cooking techniques, smartphone technology,
the location of the narwhal! Share what you discover
in a blog, or over supper with a friend.

# NOVEMBER 14 – NOVEMBER 20

*curiosity*

14 / MONDAY ○

15 / TUESDAY

16 / WEDNESDAY

NOTES

## 17 / THURSDAY

## 18 / FRIDAY

## 19 / SATURDAY

## 20 / SUNDAY

### EXPLORE FRESH IDEAS

All great things begin with an idea. One lunchtime or evening this week, organize an "ideas forum" at work or at home. Ask attendees to come along with a single idea to improve work or family life. As each person shares his or her idea, explore it together – be curious about what motivates it and what its consequences might be.

# NOVEMBER 21 – NOVEMBER 27

*curiosity*

**21 / MONDAY** ☾

**22 / TUESDAY**

**23 / WEDNESDAY** ♐

NOTES

> *"Curiosity is one of the permanent and certain characteristics of a vigorous intellect."*
>
> SAMUEL JOHNSON, ENGLISH WRITER (1709-1784)

## 24 / THURSDAY

Thanksgiving Day (USA)

## 25 / FRIDAY

## 26 / SATURDAY

## 27 / SUNDAY

First Sunday of Advent

### EXERCISE YOUR MIND

Curiosity is good exercise for the mind. On your first outdoor walk of the week, notice a specific thing in nature - the yellow centre of a daisy, the sound of a woodpecker, the particular shape of a leaf - and give yourself a mental workout by musing on why it is how it is.

# NOVEMBER OVERVIEW

| M | TU | W | TH | F | SA | SU |
|---|---|---|---|---|---|---|
| 31 | 1 | 2 | 3 | 4 | 5 | 6 |
| 7 | 8 | 9 | 10 | 11 | 12 | 13 |
| 14 | 15 | 16 | 17 | 18 | 19 | 20 |
| 21 | 22 | 23 | 24 | 25 | 26 | 27 |
| 28 | 29 | 30 | 1 | 2 | 3 | 4 |

This month I am grateful for ...

_____

_____

_____

_____

_____

_____

_____

_____

# Reflections on CURIOSITY

How did you cultivate a curious mindset this month?

_____

_____

_____

_____

_____

In what ways did becoming more curious about the world around you help you to feel more connected with and excited by your life?

_____

_____

_____

_____

_____

_____

How can you keep your curiosity alive in the future?

_____

_____

_____

_____

_____

Don't miss out on next year's diary!
See the back page for details on how to order your copies for 2017.

DECEMBER

# GROWTH

We've reached the end of the year. This is the perfect time to reflect on how we've grown, and how we can continue to grow in the year to come. One of the amazing things about life is that, although we might stop growing physically, we never, ever stop growing emotionally and mentally. There's always something to improve upon or learn more about. Spiritual, mental and emotional growth is like a blossoming tree – with each new insight, new branches of the self appear. And, over time, the tree stretches ever-upwards and sprouts blossoms of knowledge, wisdom and understanding. The activities this month will help you to review how much you've grown over the last year and look forward to all the ways in which you will continue to grow next year and forever afterwards.

### AFFIRMATION OF THE MONTH
*I am, and always will be, growing*

# NOVEMBER 28 – DECEMBER 4

*growth*

**28 / MONDAY**

**29 / TUESDAY** ●

**30 / WEDNESDAY**

St Andrew's Day observed (SCO)

NOTES

> "What makes night within us may leave stars."
>
> VICTOR HUGO, FRENCH WRITER (1802-1885)

## 1 / THURSDAY

World AIDS Day

---
---
---
---
---
---
---
---
---
---

## 2 / FRIDAY

---
---
---
---
---
---
---
---
---
---

## 3 / SATURDAY

---
---
---
---

## 4 / SUNDAY

---
---
---
---
---
---

### SEE THE STARS

Without the dark we wouldn't be able to see the beauty of the stars. Reflect on a difficult situation you've experienced this year. Then, list three lessons you learned from it, and note how these helped you to grow into the person you are now. Remind yourself to look for the stars in your experience the next time you find yourself in the dark.

# DECEMBER 5 – DECEMBER 11

*growth*

5 / MONDAY

6 / TUESDAY

7 / WEDNESDAY ☽

NOTES

*"I want to be as idle as I can, so that my soul may have time to grow."*

ELIZABETH VON ARNIM, BRITISH NOVELIST (1866-1941)

## 8 / THURSDAY

Bodhi Day (Buddha's
Enlightenment) in some countries

_____

_____

_____

_____

_____

## 9 / FRIDAY

_____

_____

_____

_____

_____

_____

_____

_____

_____

_____

## 10 / SATURDAY

_____

_____

_____

_____

## 11 / SUNDAY

_____

_____

_____

_____

_____

### EMBRACE IDLENESS

With so much to do, we often feel idleness is a
luxury we can't afford. But idle moments provide
opportunities to ponder things we might otherwise
ignore. Spend one hour this week without any
distractions. Sit outside or in your favourite place
in your home and do absolutely nothing.

# DECEMBER 12 – DECEMBER 18

*growth*

12 / MONDAY

13 / TUESDAY

14 / WEDNESDAY ○

NOTES

*"All growth is a leap in the dark."*

HENRY MILLER, AMERICAN WRITER (1891-1980)

15 / THURSDAY

16 / FRIDAY

17 / SATURDAY

18 / SUNDAY

## HAVE AN ADVENTURE

In order to grow we need to step outside routine and do things we've never done before. One day this weekend, have a mini adventure: take a different path in the woods; visit a holy place for a faith different from your own; shop on the high street rather than in the superstore. Enjoy the adventure!

# DECEMBER 19 - DECEMBER 25

*growth*

### 19 / MONDAY

### 20 / TUESDAY

### 21 / WEDNESDAY ☾

Winter Solstice
Summer Solstice (AUS, NZ)

### NOTES

> "The risk to remain tight in a bud was more painful than the risk it took to blossom."
>
> ANAÏS NIN, FRENCH AUTHOR (1903-1977)

## 22 / THURSDAY

_____

_____

_____

_____

_____

_____

_____

_____

_____

_____

_____

_____

## 23 / FRIDAY

_____

_____

_____

_____

_____

_____

_____

_____

_____

_____

_____

_____

## 24 / SATURDAY

Christmas Eve
Hanukkah begins at sundown

_____

_____

_____

## 25 / SUNDAY

Christmas Day

_____

_____

_____

_____

_____

## ENCOURAGE GROWTH

Sometimes we need to grow even when we don't want to. This week choose one aspect of your life - your career, your friendships, your romantic relationship, your emotional state - and ask yourself what three things you could do to help it grow and flourish in the future.

# DECEMBER 26 – JANUARY 1

*growth*

### 26 / MONDAY

Boxing Day
St Stephen's Day
Kwanzaa begins

### 27 / TUESDAY

### 28 / WEDNESDAY

NOTES

> "If we don't change, we don't grow.
> If we don't grow, we aren't really living."
>
> ANATOLE FRANCE, FRENCH POET (1844-1924)

## 29 / THURSDAY ●

---
---
---
---
---
---
---
---
---
---
---
---

## 30 / FRIDAY

---
---
---
---
---
---
---
---
---
---
---
---

## 31 / SATURDAY

New Year's Eve

---
---
---
---
---

## 1 / SUNDAY

New Year's Day
Kwanzaa ends

---
---
---
---

### PLAN YOUR TRANSFORMATION

Change is essential for growth. You have already changed so much in your life for the better. This week harness that positive, transformative energy and consider what more wonderful changes are to come. At the end of the week, write a list of five things you would like to change in your life in 2017.

# DECEMBER OVERVIEW

| M | TU | W | TH | F | SA | SU |
|---|----|----|----|----|----|----|
| 28 | 29 | 30 | 1 | 2 | 3 | 4 |
| 5 | 6 | 7 | 8 | 9 | 10 | 11 |
| 12 | 13 | 14 | 15 | 16 | 17 | 18 |
| 19 | 20 | 21 | 22 | 23 | 24 | 25 |
| 26 | 27 | 28 | 29 | 30 | 31 | 1 |

This month I am grateful for ...

_____

_____

_____

_____

_____

_____

_____

_____

# Reflections on GROWTH

In what ways have you grown and blossomed as a person this month? This year?

_____

_____

_____

_____

_____

_____

In what ways do you feel different - braver, stronger, bolder - than at the beginning of the year?

_____

_____

_____

_____

_____

_____

In what ways do you hope you will continue to grow during the year ahead?

_____

_____

_____

_____

_____

_____

# NOTE FROM THE AUTHOR

Hi! I'm Dani, the designer and author of this diary. Here's a bit about who I am and what I do: I'm a writer and illustrator, and the founder of PositivelyPresent.com, a website dedicated to helping people around the world live more positive and present lives. Through my website, books and illustrations I try to highlight the importance of mindfulness and making the most of every moment.

Last year, I collaborated with the Watkins team to create the first *Every Day Matters Diary*. It was such a wonderful experience that we joined up again this year so that we could continue inspiring readers and journal-lovers in 2016, too.

The last 12 months have been such an exciting time for me, not least because Watkins published my book *The Positively Present Guide to Life: How to Make the Most of Every Moment*. In it, I provide insights into how to stay positive and present in all areas of life, including at home, at work, in relationships, in love and during change.

I've really enjoyed working with the Watkins team on the diaries and my book. I hope that this enthusiasm shines through to inspire you during 2016, and even beyond. I know there are so many diaries to choose from, but I'm so glad you picked up this one.

Wishing you all the best in the year to come!